I0163127

# HOUSEHOLD GODS

## A COMEDY

BY

ALEISTER CROWLEY

*TO*

*LEILA WADDELL*

Copyright © 2018  A Yesterday's World Publishing
All rights reserved.
ISBN-13: 978-0993421068

SCENE
THE HEARTH OF CRASSUS; AFTERWARDS THE LAWNS, THE
WOODS, THE LAKE, THE ISLE.

CRASSUS, a barbarian from Britain.
ADELA, his wife, a noble Roman lady.
ALICIA, a servant in the house.
A STATUE OF PAN.
A FAUN.

# HOUSEHOLD GODS

THE SCENE *is at the hearth of* CRASSUS, *where is a little bronz* *altar dedicated to the Lares and Penates. A pale flame rises fror* *the burning sandal-wood, on which* CRASSUS *throws benzoin ar* *musk. He is standing in deep dejection.*

CRASSUS.

Smoke without fire!
  No thrill of tongues licks up
  The offerings in the cup.
Dead falls desire.

Black smoke thou art,
  O altar-flame, that dost dismember,
  Devour the hearth, to leave no ember
To warm this heart.

I see her still—
  Adela dancing here
  Till dim gods did appear
To work our will.

The delicate girl!
  Diaphanous gossamer
  Subtly revealing her
Brave breast of pearl!

Now—she's withdrawn
  At dusk to the wild woods,
  Mystic beatitudes
That dure till dawn.

Let life exclaim

Against these things of spirit,
  Mankind that disinherit
 Of love's pure flame!
[*He bends before the altar and begins to weep.*]

 Ye household gods!
  By these male tears I swear
  That ye shall grant this prayer.
All things at odds

 Shall be put straight—
  Harmonized, reconciled
  By some appointed child
 Of some far Fate!
[*A curtain has been drawn aside during this invocation, and ALICIA advances. She smiles subtly upon him; and, giving a strange gesture, makes one or two noiseless steps of dancing.*]

ALICIA.

Master still sad?

CRASSUS.
    These faint and fearful shores
 Of time are beaten by the surge of sense,
 Love worn away—by love?—to indifference.
Who knows what god—or demon—she adores?
 Or in what wood she shelters, or what grove
 Sees her profane our sacrament of love?

ALICIA.

 I saw her follow
 The stream in the hollow
 Where never Apollo
  Abides.
 So thick are the trees

3

That never the breeze
Stirs them, or sees
What satyr inhabits the glen, what nymph in the pools of it
hides.

Lighter of foot
Than a sylph or a fairy,
Sinuous, wary,
I passed from the airy
Lawns, where the flute
Of the winds made tremulous music for man.

I followed the ripple
Of the stream; I crept
Where the waters wept—
The floss in the foss
Gurgling across
The bosses of moss,
Like a dryad's nipple
In the mouth of Pan!

CRASSUS.
O pearl of the house! you came to the end?

ALICIA.
The dusk of the slave, the dawn of a friend?

CRASSUS.
Freedom is thine for the skill and the will.

ALICIA.
The skill is mine—but the will lies still,
Still as the earth that dare not stir
Till the kiss of the sun awaken her!

CRASSUS.
Yet at these secrets and riddles? Behold!
I can fill thy lap with a harvest of gold.


ALICIA.
Yet all the gold you could give to me
Would fall at my feet when I rose to be free.


CRASSUS.

What will you then?


ALICIA.
No gift from men.
Of my own free will I give you wit,
(O man so sorely in need of it!)
And happiness; and the flame that hath dwindled
On this dull hearth shall be rekindled.
But this you must swear:
To will, and to dare,
To seek the spirit and slay the sense;
  And for this hour
  To give me power
To lead you in silent obedience,
Though I bade you fall on your sword. . . .


CRASSUS.
                              Enough!
I give my life as I gave my love.


ALICIA.
O! love you have not understood.
You have not guessed its secret food.
You have not seen its single eye;
But fear and doubt and jealousy
Have risen, and now your love is trembling

Like a mountebank dissembling
When his trick's detected. Come!
To find home we must leave home.

CRASSUS.
Starless and moonless, hidden in cloud,
The night's one flame of pearl.

ALICIA.
The bat flaps; the owl hoots aloud.

CRASSUS.
Lead on; I trust you, girl.

ALICIA.
You are bold to trust me; or, have you divined
My secret?

CRASSUS.
No; the crystal of your mind
Shows only faint disturbing images,
Things passing strange, as if enchanted seas
Kept their great swell upon it, and strange fish
Played in its oily depths. Some monstrous wish,
The shadow of some unspeakable desire,
Strikes my heart cold, and sets my brain on fire.

ALICIA.
Learn this, as we pass through the portico:
Fear nothing; there is nothing you can know!
And by these terraces and steps that gleam
Wintry, although the summer night is hot,
This—what we seek is never what we find!
Life is a dream, like love; and from the dream
If we may wake, we never find it what

We would; for the wisdom of a mightier mind
Leads us in its own ways
To a perfected praise.


CRASSUS.

Why are these shadows thrown across the lawn
From the elms and yews? They were not wont to reach
Beyond the branches of that copper-beech.


ALICIA.

Attend the dawn
Of an unknown comet, that shall come
From the unfathomable wells of space
Into its halidom.


CRASSUS.

I know it not. Last night I walked alone
Here, and saw nothing.


ALICIA.
               I was not with you!
There is no God upon the eternal throne
Of stars begemming the bewildering blue
Unless one has the eyes to see him. Think
How we two stand upon the brink
Of nothing! Here's a globe, whereto we trust,
No larger than the smallest speck of dust
Or mote in the sunbeam is to that sun's self,
And we are like dead leaves in autumn's whil
Of wind upon it.


CRASSUS.
           Mystify me, girl!
It is the right of an elf.
Surely your flickering fire

Will draw me to some mire!


ALICIA.
Here the stream dips its mouth into the wood.
So does youth's calm and chaste beatitude
Touch the black mouth of Love, the ancient whore.


CRASSUS.
Girl! what a scorpion leaping from your lips!


ALICIA.
My mouth stings as no scorpion ever stang.
in this round impudent smiling face of mine
There is a poison fiercer than all wine;
And from these eyes more subtle sorrows pour
Than you can dream. These teeth have been at grips
With gods; I have sung what no girl ever sang.
These ears have heard
An insufferable word!


CRASSUS.
What do you mean?


ALICIA.
The secret's in a kiss.
Here are no kisses. Here great Artemis
Rules; only in the woodland may a man
Hide his eyes from her, pledge himself to Pan.
Come! through the tangled arches
Of cypresses and larches,
Stoop; under Artemis we walked upright;
But this is Pan's home, and the House of Night.
                    [*They enter the wood.*

CRASSUS.

So when I stoop, my cheek comes close to yours.
Give me a kiss.

ALICIA.

The poisonous apple lures
Thus the boy's mouth.   Beware!

CRASSUS.

O you are fair!
Fairer than ever! In this tangle of trees
Your hot breath wraps you in perfume.

ALICIA.

There is some gloom or doom,
A bitter harsh ingredient
In these my sorceries
Of animal scent.

CRASSUS.

Yes! there is fear mixed with the fascination.
It is the reverence that chastity, be sure!
Gains from the impure.

ALICIA.

O virtuous nation!
It is the fear of the uninitiate
Before the throne of Fate
The hierophant.

CRASSUS.

Kiss me, however!

ALICIA.
Did I grant

This favour, all were lost. It is your truth
To Adela that tempts my youth.
              [*Henceforth* ALICIA *shakes with silent laughter.*

                              CRASSUS.
What little breasts you have!

                              ALICIA.
                    Ay, maiden breasts!
Would you betray my oath?

                              CRASSUS.
                    My will contests
My wishes.

                              ALICIA.
Wait, and you shall surely see
Part of the secret that ensorcels me.
See all these bosses! It is not
As if a Titan smote himself into the earth,
And was caught into her, made one with her?

                              CRASSUS.
The scent is fierce and hot
Like a rutting panther's slot.
Yet you are matched with mirth,
Shaking each other like two wrestlers.

                              ALICIA.
                    What should stir
Your melancholy but laughter?

                              CRASSUS.
Look, before us
Light streams, a tremulous chorus.

Oh, it is vague and vacillating!

ALICIA.

Love,

Young love of maidens, is the soul thereof.
And in the midst, behold, O man!
The image of great Pan.

CRASSUS.

I fear him.

ALICIA.

Go and lie there, at his feet.
Lie supine! Lie on that moss-covered root,
While I draw forth the flute
And make a marvellous music.

[*She ceases laughing and begins to play.*

CRASSUS.

O I writhe

Beneath the force of lips, of fingers lithe
That touch the delicate stops so delicately.

ALICIA.

Hush!

I have drawn the bird from the bush.
Pan will appear anon.

CRASSUS.

Ah! Ah! . . . Ah! Ah!

ALICIA.

This music moves you. Now I'll play a tune
That would make mad the melancholy moon.

This.

CRASSUS.
Ah! you tear my soul out with the trills.
Your fingers play like summer lightning on the shaft.
It is like a storm on the mountains when it shrills;
Like the angry sea when it booms. Hark!

ALICIA.
                              Some god laughed.

CRASSUS.
Your mouth is like some god's It burns and blooms
With fire unheard of, with unguessed perfumes.
O let me kiss you!

ALICIA.
So you stop my song!                    [*She ceases the tune.*

CRASSUS.
There is another song.

ALICIA.
You do me wrong.
For you love Adela!

CRASSUS.
                    By God, girl, no!
I love Alicia.

ALICIA.
            Ah! you love her *so*!    [*She laughs*

CRASSUS.
Your laugh is shocking—why do you mock me, dear?

ALICIA.

Because you will not guess my secret here.
But—put your arms about my neck, and swear
You love me, and will always keep them there.
Then I might dare.


CRASSUS.

I swear it. O my sweet!


ALICIA.
                Then take my kiss.


CRASSUS.

Your mouth is like a rose of fire. But what is this?
I cannot bear it.


ALICIA.
                Ai! Uhu! Uhu!

It is my heart; this arrow strikes me through.
Stir not one muscle for a moment. Death!
You beast, you kill me with your urgent breath.


CRASSUS.

O how I love you!                *[He moves violently.*


ALICIA.

Fool! Now all my pain
Must be gone through again.
It is sure your chastity's unstained by crime;
You do the wrong thing just at the right time!


CRASSUS.

Why do you taunt me? All the wood is spring's,
And love is hovering o'er us with his wings.

ALICIA.

Sub pennis, penis!

CRASSUS.
Hush! you break the spell.

ALICIA.
Oh! you great fools of men, I know you well.
But nothing is so detrimental
To love as to be sentimental.
I will yet make you wise.
Know that I have the magic to disguise
Myself in many ways. Do you feel this?
(Lie still, this heaven were ruined by a kiss!)
I am a butterfly, such idle flitting
As to a flower like you is fitting
Now I'm a mole. Do you think you know me now?
Here is the earthworm severed by the plough.

CRASSUS.
You are a witch. I want your love; you give
Only love's comedy.

ALICIA.
The way to live
Is to find comedy and tragedy
In everything. But if you cannot see
Through to the Bacchanal spirit, this should suit.
Here is the blacksmith hammering a flute.

CRASSUS.
Oh love, love, kiss me!

ALICIA.
I will forge a ring

Of bloom of blood-kisses upon your neck,
Till it is like a garden of roses in late spring.

CRASSUS.
"Soft, and stung softly, fairer for a fleck."

ALICIA.
O marvellous nation!
Vanity, dullness, slobber, and quotation!

CRASSUS.
Why do you love me if you scorn me so?

ALICIA.
Why, did I say I loved you? I say no.

CRASSUS.
Why do you make love?

ALICIA.
                    To beguile the hour;
To crown my rose-wreath with a greener flower;
To do my master's bidding, that's to give
Life to yourself, who only think you live.
But listen! Have you seen the nine waves roll
Monotonous upon the shoal,
Rising and falling like a maiden asleep;
Then with a lift and a leap
The ninth wave curls, and breaks upon the beach,
And rushes up it, swallowing the sand?
I am that ocean. . . . Now, you understand?

CRASSUS.
Alicia! O! this is unbearable.
Surely this wave washes the shore of hell!

ALICIA.

Each follows each
Remorseless and indifferent as Nature
Is to each creature.

CRASSUS.

Wonderful, wonderful woman!
                    [*She throws her head back, and laughs.*

ALICIA.
                              Now, you think
You know my secret. I have given you drink,
And you are wise. But hush! to all emotion
Save this the pulse and swell of Ocean
For at the last with mouth and fingers wried
All must proclaim the triumph of the tide.

CRASSUS.

Ah! still you mock me with your cruel laugh.

ALICIA.

It is your foolish epitaph.

CRASSUS.

But this can be no mockery. Heave and sway
And curl and thrust—these waves are not at play.

ALICIA.

You feel the ocean breaking on the shoal;
But passionless and moveless is its soul.

CRASSUS.

Ah! but your soul is in your breath.

ALICIA.

Only as the graven image of death
Which men call life, and ignorantly adore!


CRASSUS.

Spare me! I cannot bear you more.


ALICIA.

Then will I drown you. Lock your fingers fast
In mind, and let our mouths mix at the last.
                    [*The statue of* PAN *is seen to be alive.*


PAN.

Shrill, shrill
Over the hill!
The hunter is hot—this is the kill!
Scream! Scream!
Dissolving the dream
Of life, the knife to the heart of the wife!
The fountain jets
Its flood of blood,
And the moss that it wets
Is an amethyst flame of violets.

Who shall escape
Murder and rape
What I am alive in my solemn shape?
Shrill, shrill,
Over the hill!
The hunter is hot—this is the kill!
The heart of the home
Is a fury of foam;
The storm is awake, and the billows comb.
But though I be
Their frenzy of glee,

I am also the passionless soul of the sea!

Mine eyes glint fire,
And my cruel lips curl;
Mine the desire
Of the god and the girl;
But fierier and fleeter,
And subtler and sweeter
Than the race of the rhythm, the march of the metre,
Is the shrilling, shrilling
Of the knife in the killing
That ends, when it must,
(O the throb and the thrust!)
In a death, in the dust,
The silence, the stillness, of satiate lust,
The solemn pause
When the veil withdraws
And man looks on his god, on the Causeless Cause.
Still, still,
Under the hill!
The hunter is dead—this is the kill!

CRASSUS.

Pan spoke.

ALICIA.
Pan never speaks till man is dumb,
And only then if he be like a child
Silently curled within its mother's womb,
Or feeding at her breast. There is a wild
Way also—when his dumbness is of death.
And there's a first and second death. Remember
To die so that no god's or angel's breath
May quicken into life the wasted ember!

CRASSUS.

I am dead now.

ALICIA.
But I must raise you up.
The night grows darker; all Pan's light is gone,
And you and I are pledged to sup
Upon a secret.

CRASSUS.
All your secret shone.
*[She laughs again.*

ALICIA.
Oh, when you know it! But you must divine
Adela's shrine.

CRASSUS.
I am weary of Adela grown chaste and chill.

ALICIA.
The hunter lags; how heavy is the hill!
But you are bound to Adela.

CRASSUS.
To you!

ALICIA.
But you have given me freedom.   I will leave you.

CRASSUS.
What have I done to grieve you?

ALICIA.
You have been the solemn fool with face awry

That I have gathered in my ecstasy.
You are only a vulgar primrose I have plucked.

CRASSUS.
At least, she-devil, you have been well—treated.

ALICIA.
O tragic farce—not even rimes completed!
Nay, darling! no rebellion. When you know
My secret, you will understand. You are bound
To Adela within the portico,
To me upon this ground.
By day, in life, adore the Lares, man!
By night, in death, make offering to Pan!
Can you cut day from night by any endeavour?
If so, both life and death were lost for ever.
Come, the stream steepens.

CRASSUS.
This road leads to hell.

ALICIA.
The way to heaven is shorter.

CRASSUS.
Who can tell?

ALICIA.
I have measured it.

CRASSUS.
You, girl?

ALICIA.
It is not hard.

CRASSUS.
What did you make the height of it?

ALICIA.
One yard.

CRASSUS.
You always mock me?

ALICIA.
Pity of my youth!
I swerve not from, you stumble at, the truth.

CRASSUS.
I like not jests.   This is a serious journey.

ALICIA.
Why did you make a mocker your attorney?
The way to Rome leads through the Apennines.
Bacchus has horns beneath the crown of vines.
If you fear horns, make some polite excuse
Not to invoke him by the name Zagreus!

A FAUN [*Passing among the trees*].
Ye thought me a lamb
  With a crown of thorns;
 I am royal, a ram
  With death in my horns.
 So mild and soft
  And feminine,
 Ye held me aloft
  And frowned on sin!
 But I was awake
  In your clasp as I lay;
 I roused the snake

From its nest of clay;
And ere ye knew
  I had sunk my forehead
Through and through;
  Harsh and horrid
Through all the pleasure
  Of rose and vine
I thrust my treasure,
  The cone of the pine.
Irru's maid
  Was easily sated,
For she was afraid
  When Irru mated!

CRASSUS.

Ha! Ha! Ha! Ha! Ha! Ha!

ALICIA.

               You would not laugh

Were you the maid!

CRASSUS.
How could I be?

ALICIA.

                  Great calf!

But you are all the same, blaspheme and jeer
At any mystery beyond your sphere
Of beer, and beef, and beer, and beef, and beer.
Now you have frightened the shy god!

CRASSUS.

                 Why heed?

Between your—arms—is all the god I need.

ALICIA.
Prudish and coarse to the last. Now hush indeed!
The stream kisses the lake. We near the shrine.
Stir no snapped twig. Let your foot—even yours—
Fall like a fawn's.

CRASSUS.
Your breath is like new wine.

ALICIA.
Hush now! no porpoise gambols!

CRASSUS.
How obscure's
The glimmer of the lake.  Is that the isle?

ALICIA.
Yes! in that shadow lurks a smile.
See; from that jagged cloud Diana starts
Like a deer from the brake; her silver splendour darts
Through the crisp air to the grove upon the isle. . .
Do you see her? Do you see her?

CRASSUS.
Monstrous! Vile!
These eyes betray me.

ALICIA.
No! your Adela lies
With arms thrown back, head tilted, open thighs.
Her lips flame out like poppies in the dusk.
The breeze brings back to us a scent of musk.
Her mouth is oozing kisses!

CRASSUS.
                                    Filthy harlot!

ALICIA.
I never fed on a superber scarlet.
And look! the wonder of plumes that foams upon
Her tidal breast—oh, but a swan! a swan!
A swan snow-white with his sole scarlet hidden
In the abode forbidden!
O but his eye swoons as his broad beak slips
Within her luscious lips.
O but—I cannot see—I long to die
Alike for wonder—and for jealousy!

CRASSUS.
Vile, filthy whore! I'll catch you at it.

ALICIA.
                                              Soft!
See how his feathers hold her soul aloft!

CRASSUS.
Beast! Have you brought me through the wood for this?

ALICIA.
No wonder I must teach you how to kiss.

CRASSUS.
I'll clip his wings.

ALICIA.
        Sub pennis, penis! 'Slife!
It's not the wings of him that clip your wife.

CRASSUS.
Thou art as filthy a creature as she!

ALICIA.
Fat fool!
All your emotions vary with your——

CRASSUS.
What?

ALICIA.
Your state of health.

CRASSUS.
Be off with you, foul——

ALICIA.
Well?

CRASSUS.
I'll swim and stab them. The black mouth of hell
Yawns for their murder.

ALICIA.
I'll be at the death.
Dive then, but softly. Scarcely draw your breath.

CRASSUS.
O, she's unwary!

ALICIA.
Is your love forgotten?

CRASSUS.
All love is rotten.

ALICIA.
But your pure love for me you boasted of?

CRASSUS.
Ay, that was perfect love.

ALICIA.
You love me then, not her?

CRASSUS.
Indeed I do.

ALICIA.
Swear me the oath anew!

CRASSUS.
I swear to love you till the world shall end.

ALICIA.
Then, Crassus, I will always be your friend.

CRASSUS.
Ah, that is good! You do not mock me now!

ALICIA.
Creep softly to the land. Kiss but my brow.
My curls are wet. . . . No, never touch me there!

CRASSUS.
Why? Have I not?

ALICIA.
You have not.

CRASSUS.

                          Just my hand.

ALICIA.

You disobey your mistress's command?
The time is near when you shall see
The keyhole of my comedy!

CRASSUS.

Ha! Ha! Ha!

ALICIA.

Hush, you coarse slave; we'll surprise
Your good wife in her mystic exercise.
Quick, through the bramble!
                     *[They burst through upon* ADELA.

CRASSUS.

                Now, you beast, I've got you!
The curst of God, and plague of Naples, rot you!
For this white brute—one slit!
            *[He cuts the throat of* THE SWAN *with his dagger.*

ADELA.

                Oh love betrayed!
O my dead beauty! Faugh! deceitful maid.
Not Crassus found me out. Had I the wings
Of my dead love—oh love!——

ALICIA.

                Why, wondrous things!

ADELA.

These nails shall serve. A servant!

CRASSUS.
                                    She shall be
My wife, damned witch, when I have done with thee!
                              [THE SWAN *dies.*


ADELA.
I'll kill her now. But see! my swan is dead.


ALICIA.
Yes! and what light is breaking overhead?
What blaze of blue and gold envelops us?


CRASSUS.
O marvel! O miraculous!


ADELA.
What is it? Why, my lover's life, in me
Once concentrated, now diffused, illumes
The endless reaches of eternity
With infinite brilliance, with intense perfumes.


ALICIA.
O then your lover was some god's disguise.


ADELA.
And you have robbed me. Now beware your eyes!
              [*She springs at* ALICIA, *who guards herself easily. But*
                    *in the struggle her robe tears.*


ALICIA.
Take care!


ADELA.
            A boy!

CRASSUS.
A boy! Then what am I?

ALICIA.
That is the key-word of the comedy.
You thought you had two vices at your need;
But she had Jove and you had Ganymede.
    [*They are struck dumb and still with amazement.* ALICIA *claps
       her hands four times.*

Sweep through the air, bright blaze of eagle-wings!
Crassus, sub pennis, penis! How he swings
His bulk from yonder sightless poise, to bear
me back to the Dominion of the air
Where I shall bear the cup of Jupiter!
Blind babes, love one another, no less true
Because the gods have deigned to dwell with you!
                [*The eagle bears* GANYMEDE *aloft.*

CRASSUS.
Adela! these mysteries too great
For you and me to estimate.
But, widowed both, come, seek domestic charms
As we were wont, in one another's arms!
What perfect moss for you to lie upon!

ADELA.
I am your wife, dear Crassus.
         (*sotto voce*) Oh, my swan!

CURTAIN.

www.ingramcontent.com/pod-product-compliance
Lightning Source LLC
Chambersburg PA
CBHW060106050426
42448CD00011B/2636

* 9 7 8 0 9 9 3 4 2 1 0 6 8 *